The Experts

KOOKOGEY™

NASHVILLE

Copyright © 2010 by Kevin S. Kookogey

All rights reserved. No part of this book may be reproduced or transmitted in whole or in part in any form or by any means, including, without limitation, electronically or mechanically, including photocopying, recording, or via any form of information storage and retrieval system, without permission in writing from the publisher.

Published by THE KOOKOGEY GROUP, 9050 Carothers Pkwy, Suite 104, #25, Franklin, TN 37067

www.kookogey.com

The KOOKOGEY name and logo are trademarks of THE KOOKOGEY GROUP, registration pending in the United States Patent & Trademark Office.

Kevin Kookogey is an entertainment lawyer who speaks and teaches on topics as diverse as music and entertainment, politics, western civilization and education. For more information or to book Mr. Kookogey for an event, please contact kevin@thekookogeygroup.com, or visit our website at www.kookogey.com

Cover Design by Kevin Kookogey and Marc Theodosiou

Illustrations by Chris Taylor

Art Direction by Kevin Kookogey
Special thanks to Jordan Mattison

9050 Carothers Pkwy, Suite 104 #25, Franklin, TN 37067

Manufactured in the United States of America

ISBN: 978-0-615-40231-4

To all good men who have replaced true Religion with their worship of the State; who have abandoned curiosity; who have ascribed moral superiority to the Government despite its aims to control freedom and happiness; who have eschewed self-reliance in favor of dependence on a panel of administrative Geniuses; Who have allowed all sorts of Evil in the name of Peace.
 I give you ...

The Experts

In search of perfection...

The facts they ignore

In hopes you'll believe
we've not seen this before

"Extreme situations they are," and therefore

There must be more central control

In search of perfection
the past is outgrown

Destroying tradition, remaking their own

A "crisis" requires
a great Chaperone

There must be more central control

In search of perfection
their mandates increase

Redoubling pursuit of chimerical peace

"Injustice" requires
that freedom decrease

The hope of more central control

In search of perfection,
don't make a mistake

They'll nationalize
ev'ry profit you make

And everything else
"for the good" they will take

To realize central control

In search of perfection
the king condescends

With words and more words
and more words he pretends

We are making history!
Business can't be trusted!
I inherited all of my problems!
I didn't know!
It has never been worse than this!
I am in charge... really I am... I mean it!
Unparalleled circumstances!
Let me be clear!
I need to know whose ass to kick!

SEAL of the EXPERT in CHIEF

Unconscionable means justified by the ends

Of gaining more central control

In search of perfection
they lecture us more

- We have commissioned a panel of experts...
  - We have graduated from important schools...
- Despite how you feel, times are good- uh, at least for me & my Government homeboys.
- The only legitimate means of expressing compassion is through the state.

Convinced they're the ones
that we've been waiting for

Intent on utopian
dreams to restore

And seizing more central control

In search of perfection
they're propped on a perch

While casting aspersions;
good names they besmirch

The harshest contempt
they reserve for the Church

While worshipping Central Control

In search of perfection,
there's no need to vote

With freedom secured
by a boot to the throat

And no need for Virtue,
for risk is remote

The fruits of more central control

In search of perfection,
the ones who know best

From ivory towers
in bowtie and vest

Pontificate smugly disdain for the West

Self-righteous with central control

In search of perfection,
it's all within reach

The climate, your health, and political speech

Ignore your Religion
and what it may teach

Salvation is central control

In search of perfection
restrained not a spec

These planners proceed without balance or check

The heirs of Rousseau bleed contempt for Hayek

And dream of more central control

In search of perfection,
we all rest secure

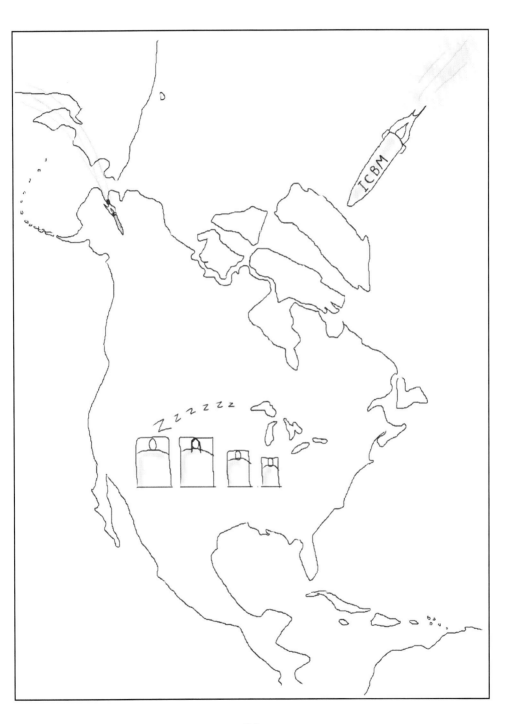

The Government's motives
are certainly pure

If not for the curious
they could assure

Fulfillment through central control

In search of perfection,
they spare no expense

To mete out your substance
without consequence

Concern for the poor
a parade of pretense

This vanity, Central Control

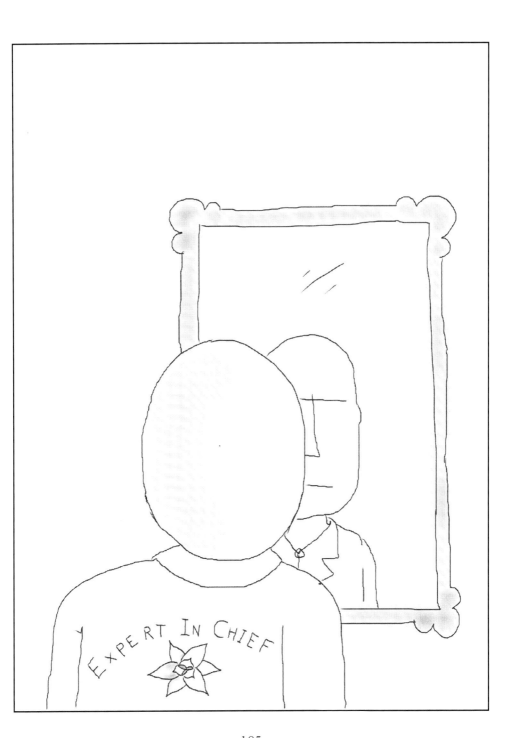

In search of perfection
they really do care

Purloining your assets for others to share

Unbending, Inflexible, Strict, Doctrinaire

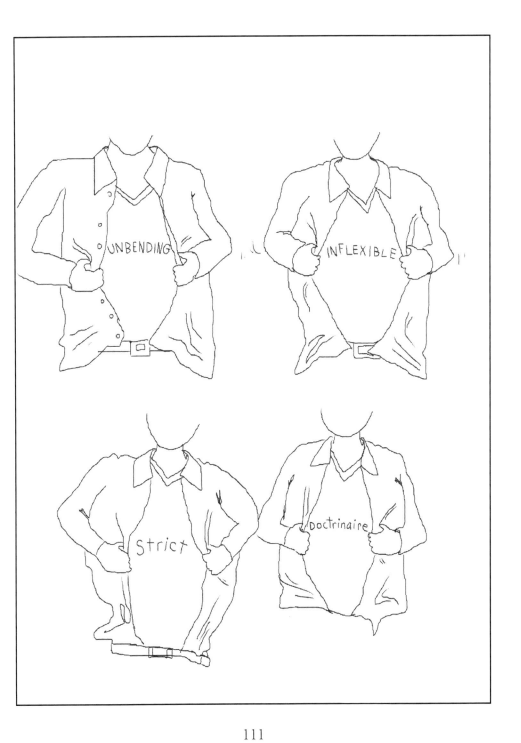

These guards of more central control

In search of perfection, increasing the hedge

The more the resistance
the harder the edge

"It's all for your good,"
and "We care!" they allege

Obsessed with more central control

In search of perfection,
they war through the night

With Peace a disguise
for a radical fight

For all that is wrong
against all that is right

The cure is more central control

In search of perfection,
contending in vain

Against the unchangeable,
blindly they strain

For year after year,
from campaign to campaign

Relentless for Central Control

In search of perfection that doesn't exist

When argument fails
they resort to the fist

That cowardly brand
of the true atheist

Insane for more central control

In search of perfection,
they do what they do

Though never content
with the ends they pursue

The lie of the false
is that True isn't true

The End of all Central Control

In search of perfection,
the battle is done

Resign your defenses,
the Experts have won

Consigned to the dust bin of History, my son

The Experts

In search of perfection the facts they ignore
In hopes you'll believe we've not seen this before
"Extreme situations they are," and therefore
There must be more central control

In search of perfection the past is outgrown
Destroying tradition, remaking their own
A "crisis" requires a great Chaperone
There must be more central control

In search of perfection their mandates increase
Redoubling pursuit of chimerical peace
"Injustice" requires that freedom decrease
The hope of more central control

In search of perfection, don't make a mistake
They'll nationalize ev'ry profit you make
And everything else "for the good" they will take
To realize central control

In search of perfection the king condescends
With words and more words and more words he pretends
Unconscionable means justified by the ends
Of gaining more central control

In search of perfection they lecture us more
Convinced they're the ones that we've been waiting for
Intent on utopian dreams to restore
And seizing more central control

In search of perfection they're propped on a perch
While casting aspersions; good names they besmirch
The harshest contempt they reserve for the Church
While worshipping Central Control

In search of perfection, there's no need to vote
With freedom secured by a boot to the throat
And no need for Virtue, for risk is remote
The fruits of more central control

In search of perfection, the ones who know best
From ivory towers in bowtie and vest
Pontificate smugly disdain for the West
Self-righteous with central control

In search of perfection, it's all within reach
The climate, your health, and political speech
Ignore your Religion and what it may teach
Salvation is central control

In search of perfection restrained not a spec
These planners proceed without balance or check
The heirs of Rousseau bleed contempt for Hayek
And dream of more central control

In search of perfection, we all rest secure
The Government's motives are certainly pure
If not for the curious they could assure
Fulfillment through central control

In search of perfection, they spare no expense
To mete out your substance without consequence
Concern for the poor a parade of pretense
This vanity, Central Control

In search of perfection they really do care
Purloining your assets for others to share
Unbending, inflexible, strict, doctrinaire
These guards of more central control

In search of perfection, increasing the hedge
The more the resistance the harder the edge
"It's all for your good," and "We care!" they allege
Obsessed with more central control

In search of perfection, they war through the night
With Peace a disguise for a radical fight
For all that is wrong against all that is right
The cure is more central control

In search of perfection, contending in vain
Against the unchangeable, blindly they strain
For year after year, from campaign to campaign
Relentless for Central Control

In search of perfection that doesn't exist
When argument fails they resort to the fist
That cowardly brand of the true atheist
Insane for more central control

In search of perfection, they do what they do
Though never content with the ends they pursue
The lie of the false is that True isn't true
The End of all Central Control

In search of perfection, the battle is done
Resign your defenses, the Experts have won
Consigned to the dust bin of History, my son

Copyright © 2010 by Kevin S. Kookogey

Made in the USA
Charleston, SC
21 October 2010